Marijuana: Seed To Weed

A Beginner's Guide To Planting and Harvesting Your Cannabis

Joseph J. Miller

© 2016

Disclaimer

All rights reserved. No part of this publication may be reproduced, distributed, or transmitted in any form or by any means, including photocopying, recording, or other electronic or mechanical methods, without the prior written permission of the publisher, except in the case of brief quotations embodied in critical reviews and certain other noncommercial uses permitted by copyright law.

This book is not intended as a substitute for the medical advice of physicians. The reader should regularly consult a physician in matters relating to his/her health and particularly with respect to any symptoms that may require diagnosis or medical attention.

Table of Contents

Introduction 5
Brief History 6
Medical Uses 8
Legalization & Cultivation Opportunities 9
Types Of Cannabis And Differences In Each 11
Why Cannabis Is Considered Valuable 12
    a) Cannabinoids: 12
        a) Tetrahydrocannabinol (THC): 12
        b) Cannabidiol (CBD): 12
        c) Cannabinol (CBN): 12
        d) Cannabigerol (CBG): 12
        e) Cannabichromene (CBC): 12
    b) Terpenoids: 13
        a) B-Caryophyllene 13
        b) Terpinolene: 13
        c) Limonene: 13
        d) Myrcene: 13
        e) Linalool: 13
Anatomy of The Cannabis Plant 14
Indoor Cultivation Of Cannabis 17
    Controlled Growing Environments For Cannabis 17
    The Growing Environment: 17
        a) Space & Reflective Coverings: 17
        b) Grow Mediums: 18
        c) Lights & Reflective Hoods: 19
        d) Electricity and Wiring: 20
        e) Water: 20
        f) Ventilation: 21

- g) Timers: 22
- h) Thermometers: 22
- i) Pests and disease: 22
- Additional Caution: 23
- Determining The Species 24

Obtaining Seeds 25
- Germinating Cannabis Seeds 25
  - Sprouting Method 1: 25
  - Sprouting Method 2: 25
  - Sprouting Method 3: 25
- Alternative Sprouting Method: Clones i.e. Cuttings 26
  - Determining The Sex Of A Cannabis Plant (Method 1): 27
  - Determining The Sex Of A Cannabis Plant (Method 2): 27

Growth Cycle Of The Cannabis Plant 29
- Seedling 29
- Vegetative Stage 30
- Flowering/ Budding/ Blooming 30
- Harvest 30

Cultivating Cannabis Through Hydroponics 32
Outdoor Cannabis Cultivation 34
Conclusion 37
Endnotes 38
Works Cited 40

Introduction

Halfway into the 2010 - 2020, a major milestone was recorded as the world witnessed the landmark legalization of cannabis use. Prior to the legalization of cannabis, most growers kept their activities secret for very obvious reasons. Even the most basic cultivation techniques were highly kept secrets and the most complex secrets remained shrouded in mystery.

The legalization of the use and cultivation of cannabis has not only opened several opportunities in the emerging cannabis cultivation industry for production and sale of cannabis, it has also ignited the quest to bridge the knowledge gap that newcomers into the industry require in order to breed higher quality plants.

As the cannabis industry matures, the demand for this technical knowledge intensifies. As expected, the major growers are focusing on increasing production volumes and cashing in on the potential profits. However, a number of growers, particularly those who have benefitted from collaboration, experimented and succeeded through trial and error are beginning to share their knowledge of how to grow cannabis.

Brief History

Ancient historical records of Shennong who was the Emperor of China about 5,000 years ago[1] contains various medicinal uses of marijuana, which the Emperor himself frequently used. It included claims of marijuana being able to cure ailments like malaria, gout, and mild amnesia. The Indians also used cannabis a lot, particularly for recreational purposes. By 500 AD, recreational use of cannabis had spread to Europe.

In the Middle East where Islam is the predominant religion, alcohol use is banned. The use of 'hashish'[2], a solid or powdered form of cannabis plant resins which is smoked through long heated pipes or vaporizers[3], is an accepted form of recreation. Smoking hashish is also prevalent in Persia and North Africa.

By the fifteenth and sixteenth centuries, cannabis was introduced to Spain and America respectively. In America, cannabis was extensively cultivated and its fiber was used for everyday items like cloth, ropes and paper. Two American presidents, George Washington and Thomas Jefferson were cannabis farmers and it is on record that the paper on which Jefferson wrote the American Declaration of Independence was made from cannabis and the first ever flag of America was also woven from fibers from the cannabis plant.

Pharmacies in eighteenth and nineteenth century America listed cannabis as medication, which could help relieve arthritis pain, suppress nausea and even reduce childbearing pain.

Immigrants, who arrived in America following the Mexican Revolution in the nineteenth century, were also said to have popularized cannabis use for recreational purpose. This stirred up a lot of anti-immigrant sentiments, which threw the crop in a bad light, as it had already been overshadowed by cotton as a more profitable cash crop for American farmers. Slowly but surely, sentiments began to rise strongly against the use of cannabis. By the year 1913, the state of California became the first to ban the use of cannabis.

Despite the disgruntlement brewing about the use of cannabis, many American musicians and show business people still popularized its used which led to recreational joints disguised as clubs called 'teapads' springing up in several places around the country. Though in most parts of America then, cannabis was not outlawed, but the teapads provided avenues for relationships between Americans of different races to mingle and socialize.

Campaigns against cannabis use started rising once again by the largely Caucasian authorities to curtail what they termed as 'breakdown of social order'. The United States Drug Enforcement Authority stated that cannabis use was addictive and could act as a gateway to other stronger narcotic drugs.[4] Most of these happened in the 1930's. In 1937, the United States Congress passed the Marijuana Tax Act which criminalized the use of cannabis, but by the 1950's, cannabis use was steadily gaining ground again then the hippie movement fueled cannabis use by the 1960's. Cannabis was now a symbol for thousands of non-conformist, American youths rebelling against the government.

The US Congress swung into action and classified cannabis, alongside other hard substances like heroin as 'Schedule 1' i.e. hard drugs in the 1972's 'Controlled Substances Act'. Critics of the act say that subsequent United States governments who applied the act strictly prompted a surge of arrests and eventual overpopulation of prisons. Most of the possession offenders were from ethnic minorities like Hispanics and African Americans. A good number of them were not guilty of violent crimes.

Other governments like Mexico followed America's stance by destroying all cannabis plants in its country. Drug cartels in countries like Colombia capitalized on these laws and intensified their operations making the country a major cannabis supplier.

By the 1990s, California, once again, became the first state to legalize the use of cannabis for medical purposes. A number of states followed suit, but this gradually increases when countless celebrities and at this point, up to three United States Presidents[5] had all admitted to using cannabis.

April 20th is now celebrated as 'International Marijuana Day' and, at least, twenty-three states in America have legalized the use of cannabis for medicinal purposes only. A few have approved it for recreational purposes. With Uruguay being the first country in the world to fully legalize the use of cannabis, in 2013; it seems it will not be too long before other countries start following suit.

Medical Uses

For the last 3,000 years, cannabis has been used medicinally in traditional medication. With the advances in scientific testing, a lot of previous medicinal applications of the plant have been verified to be true and more uses are being identified.

There are several medical uses to which cannabis has been recommended. Historically, it is said to be an efficient pain reliever. It helps with painful ailments like arthritis and even labor pain during childbirth. It is also effective for reducing nausea.

Cannabis is also effective in relieving some symptoms of HIV and cancer. Cannabis has also been said to be able to reduce cholesterol in the bloodstream. It can also help reduce fat deposits around organs like the liver. These properties help people with type two diabetes. Additionally, THCV, a compound found in cannabis, helps increase sensitivity to insulin and at the same time, protect the insulin-producing cells in the body by forming a protective layer around it. THCV also increases productivity and longevity in insulin-producing cells.

Some compounds in cannabis are can suppress appetite for a short period but are being researched for possible usefulness in obesity management. Cannabinoids found in cannabis possess muscle-relaxing properties and there are already trials to see if they could offer possible solutions for problems like epilepsy and multiple sclerosis.

Cannabis can be consumed in three major ways. It can be inhaled, taken orally or applied topically. The most potent delivery method is through inhalation and there are several ways it can be inhaled. Most episodes of cannabis-induced psychosis usually occur when cannabis is taken through inhalation. Pipes, rolls or the more modern vaporizers, offer different ways through which cannabis can be inhaled. It can be taken orally in liquid or capsule forms. Usually, topical applications of cannabis are usually for localized pain and the cannabis oil is mixed with a carrier oil like coconut, almond or olive oil before it is applied topically. Topical applications are the least potent.

Legalization & Cultivation Opportunities

Use of cannabis, whether for general or recreational purposes is governed by the law. Any user or grower will need to take up the responsibility to check the laws surrounding cannabis use in the area they use or cultivate it and cannabis laws, like other laws, can be gotten from the public domain. Some countries are liberal and some are not. Countries that are liberal about cannabis use are still in the minority but a good number of countries have decriminalized its use so possessing it is not regarded as a criminal offense.

Penalties for being in possession of cannabis range from being extremely punitive to a slap on the wrist to the absence of a penalty depending on the country the possessor lives in. Possessors can earn the death penalty in some countries. In several countries around the globe, legalizing cannabis has stirred the hornet's nest.

Between the 1930s and 1940s in the United States, prohibitions on cannabis use became very rampant. Some countries have decriminalized the possession of small quantities of cannabis, for example, North America, South America, and Europe. Furthermore, possession is legal or effectively legal in the Netherlands, North Korea, and the U.S. states of Washington and Colorado at the state level (on 28 May 2013, Colorado became the world's first fully regulated recreational cannabis market for adults). On 10 December 2013, Uruguay became the first country in the world to fully legalize the sale, production, and distribution of marijuana.

Currently in the United States, laws governing the use of cannabis vary from state to state. Four out of the entire fifty states have entirely legalized the use of cannabis for medical and recreation purposes, some have relaxed both medical and decriminalization laws relating to its use. Other states have decriminalized cannabis their possession laws and a couple more have legalized psychoactive or non-psychoactive medical cannabis. While a total of twenty-three states and Washington DC have legalized the use of cannabis in some form, about twenty-two states, and two inhabited territories totally prohibit cannabis use for any reason.

The official grower of cannabis in the United States since the year 1968 has been the University of Mississippi. With the legislature around its use for medicinal as well as recreational purposes relaxing across the United States, the demand for cannabis is increasing and along with it comes a need to fill in the supply gap. It is estimated that if cannabis is fully legalized throughout the United States of America, it could generate approximately $40 - $60 billion (USD) per annum. The industry is gathering momentum and doors are beginning to open for new cannabis farmers to fill the need of the end users of the product.

Types Of Cannabis And Differences In Each

Cannabis plants can either be male or female after some weeks of growing. The male plants pollinate the female species. After pollination, the females develop seeds, which mature, ripen and then fall to the ground.

In tropical, warmer regions like the Caribbean, Africa, Middle East and Mexico the sativa species of cannabis is more abundant. Their major characteristic is the shape of their leaves, which are usually long and thin, and their height. They are very tall cannabis plants. They also take longer to grow in comparison with other species of cannabis probably as a result of adaptation to their environment.

In temperate, colder regions like Europe, United States, Canada, etc., the indica species of cannabis is more common. The major physical characteristic of the indica variety is their broad leaves and shorter height. They also have a shorter maturity period[6]

The third strain of cannabis is the ruderalis. It contains significantly lower amounts of THC and is the least popular. This species is primarily used in the making of fabric for clothes, ropes and shoes. There are also several hybrids of the cannabis plant like the Skunk, Orange Bud, Blueberry and Northern Lights.

All strains of cannabis contain unique compounds known as cannabinoids which can be further broken down into cannabinoids and terpenoids. The sativa and indica species have different chemical compositions that make them unique. The different compounds contained in each variety and the volume of that compound will determine the various uses to which that particular species can be applied.

These compounds will determine the scent of the cannabis and the various medicinal uses which it can be utilized in. A higher level of one compound in the sativa variety might cause it to possess more psychedelic properties, while the presence of another cannabinoid in the indica variety could make it more calming. They are explained in more detail in the next section.

Why Cannabis Is Considered Valuable

When you look at a cannabis bud, there are resins that are seen on it. When examined microscopically, these resins usually look like crystals. When heated or smoked, these crystals release certain compounds. Understanding the chemical composition of these compounds will reveal why cannabis is considered valuable.

The two categories of chemicals found in cannabis are Cannabinoids and Terpenoids.

a) Cannabinoids:
These are the medicinal and psychoactive molecules which make cannabis potent and addictive. They are usually acidic before they are broken down.

a) Tetrahydrocannabinol (THC):
These are highly psychoactive cannabinoids. They have many properties including pain relief, reduce symptoms of nausea i.e. antiemetic and help with muscle spasticity

b) Cannabidiol (CBD):
This type has been found to be very useful in addressing seizures so it is used for conditions like epilepsy and multiple sclerosis. In comparison to THCs, CBDs are not psychoactive and calming. CBDs are also used to relieve stress and reduce insomnia and also for diabetes.

c) Cannabinol (CBN):
When THC is heated up, CBN is produced. Like CBD, CBN also helps with sleep disorder as like insomnia and is a very strong sedative. It also has antiemetic properties thus helps curb nausea.

d) Cannabigerol (CBG):
CBG is a precursor to THC and CBD. Like CBD, it is non-psychoactive and has a unique characteristic of being able to stimulate the growth of brain cells. The presence of CBG compounds is believed by some scientists to be necessary to achieve a full psychoactive effect during the use of cannabis.

e) Cannabichromene (CBC):
Another non-psychoactive compound which is beneficial for the treatment of anxiety and stress-related conditions. It also helps with inflammation.

b) Terpenoids:

These give each species of cannabis its own peculiar flavor and scent. Different cannabis species have their own specific terpenoids.

a) B-Caryophyllene

This terpenoid has antibacterial, antifungal and antiseptic. It is a spicy aroma which can be found in plants like cloves, black pepper, and Thai basil.

b) Terpinolene:

Terpinolene has a smoky/woody, earthy scent. For centuries, it has been used as an antiseptic.

c) Limonene:

This terpenoid emits a citrus scent and has anti-fungal properties. It is efficient in the treatment of gastric reflux.

d) Myrcene:

B-Myrcene is also found in mangoes. Cannabis users experience more intense highs if they eat a mango before using cannabis. The activities of these terpenoids are very evident in the brain. They lower blood to brain barrier resistance and also increase the maximum saturation of the brain's cannabinoid receptors.

e) Linalool:

This terpenoid is also found in plants like lavender, rosewood, birch and coriander. It is a painkiller and it is also a precursor in the production of Vitamin E. Linalool is also an effective insecticide.

Sativa varieties have the highest levels of Terpinolene. They also contain high levels of B-Myrcene. Indica species, on the other hand, contain more Linalool, Limonene, and B-Caryophyllene.

Anatomy of The Cannabis Plant

The focus of the end user is always the cannabis bud from which the medicinal properties of its resins are obtained when smoked. However, like all other plants, a good understanding of various parts of the plant will help the grower cultivate better crop yield.

Cannabis plants are dioecious. This simply means they could either be male or female. A small proportion of them are hermaphrodite actually but they are a minority.

The female cannabis plants produce the cluster of flowers, which secrete resin and are then trimmed into the buds that are usually the most sought after, higher priced and valuable part of the plant. The male cannabis plants, on the other hand, pollinate the female plants to initiate seed production but there is a catch to this.

Unpollinated female cannabis plants can also produce buds. And the cannabinoid content in the resin from the buds of an unpollinated, seedless female plant is actually very rich. Because of this proven fact, most growers aim to exclusively grow only female seedless plants. The mathematics behind this is very simple. More female seedless plants, more flowers, more flowers, more buds and this translate to more profit in the hand of the grower.

Cannabis plants also have common features like all other flowering plants. Some physical characteristics of the cannabis plant are quite different. For example, it grows on long stems and has fan-like leaves. Its leaves extend out from nodes.

There is usually a cluster from where female flowers bloom. These are known as colas. The main one (which was usually the first cola to appear) is always visible at the very top of the plant and is usually the largest cola. Smaller colas usually appear at the nodes of the plant. These colas usually start growing after the main cola appears. The main cola is sometimes called the apex cola.

With a trained or expert eye, one will be able to see that the flower on the female plant is not just one single cluster but actually is contains several tear-shaped calyx clustered together which make up the flower. Calyxes have different shapes, sizes, and colors and they secrete the cannabinoids which the end user enjoys through glands called trichomes.

There are usually tiny strands or hairs that spring out from the calyx known as pistils which have a vibrant, reddish orange color. When pistils first appear, they are white in color and later darken to hues of yellow, amber, red, orange or brown as the cannabis plant matures. Their colors make the cannabis buds look more appealing to the human eye. The pistils actually play a major reproductive role in the female cannabis plant by receiving pollen from male plants. They, however, do not have any significant effect in the determining the buds eventual potency or flavor.

Cannabis leaves, flowers, trims, hash and stems tips are used to make products like oil. The leaves are the primary ingredient but using other parts of the plant is said to add a wider spectrum to the oil.

Indoor Cultivation Of Cannabis

A larger number of commercial cannabis growers cultivate the plant indoors under controlled environments. In environments like these, desired results are more achievable and better quality end-products are easier to harvest.

Controlled Growing Environments For Cannabis

A modern farming technique like growing plants in controlled environments is a tremendous way of optimizing limited space and crop yield. Growing cannabis in a controlled environment gives the grower a number of advantages.

The major advantage is the huge amount of control over managing crop lifecycle and product quality. The grower is better able to produce plants of uniform quantity and quality within a grow room because the simulated environmental conditions for every plant is the same.

In a grow room, the grower also has the advantage of disease control because, in the eventual outbreak of any disease, he will be able to keep to a minimum and eventually eliminate it. This is done by identifying, isolating and destroying any infected plant quickly in order to curtail eventual spread, unlike a normal, outdoor grow environment.

The Growing Environment: Cannabis farmers aim to recreate all the elements of the natural environment in a grow room. A grow room is usually an indoor, enclosed space which is kept sterile and solely devoted to cultivating cannabis plants.

There are some equipment and technical implementations that are fundamentally important when setting up a grow room:

a) **Space & Reflective Coverings:** A lot of thought should be put into designing cannabis grow rooms. The general rule of thumb is to utilize an average space of one square meter per plant. This can be used to estimate the number of plants, which can be grown within any space.

The size of a grow room could range from a cupboard to a room like an entire basement or garage. Whatever the size of the room that is eventually used, it is necessary that it is an enclosure. It is also necessary that the number of cannabis plants per square meter should not be excessive such as to have overcrowding which can stunt plant growth.

If space in the grow room is underutilized, particularly when the grower is planting for commercial reasons and not for personal use, then a review of the number of seedlings planted might be necessary to augment costs expensed while setting up and maintaining the grow room.

The walls and ceilings of a grow room should be covered with reflective material or plastic. They can also be painted white. Doing this will help conserve light within the grow room. Proper lighting is one of the most important things that will determine the quality and quantity of the crop yield. It also does not come cheap. A reflective wall and ceiling will ensure light is not wasted and it is reflected back on the plants to enable them to grow to their maximum height.

If the walls and ceilings of a grow room are not covered with reflective material, the light emitted from the bulbs will be converted to heat.

b) **Grow Mediums:** A wide variety of choices are available when it comes to selecting grow mediums for cannabis plants. The most important thing is to ensure that the growing medium selected is light grow mix with soft, textured grains which can hold water and also easily drain excess water. A lot of growers prefer a soil-less mix[7]. Potting soil is also good. Both of them are easy to get.

Fertilizer is usually added to soil mixes but soilless mixes would usually be devoid of any fertilizer. It is always better to purchase plain soil mixes or soilless mixes and fertilize with the adequate amount for growing cannabis plants. Fertilizers can be mixed into soilless mixes before planting or added in liquid form later when the plant is being watered.

Use of chemical fertilizers is more common because of it is easy to use, requires basic knowledge and simple mixing techniques. They basically contain NPK[8] (Nitrogen, Potassium, and Phosphorous) which cannabis thrives on, as well as other trace nutrients which are secondary. Organic fertilizers are more complex to understand but cannabis growers who use them claim that the end product is cleaner and tastier. The end users usually cannot tell the difference.

Fertilizers must be used according to instruction. Over-fertilization is a huge temptation. During the last stage of the plants life, i.e. about two weeks before the buds are harvested, there will be absolutely no need for fertilizer. Adding fertilizer at this stage will affect the quality of the harvested buds.

Soil mixes are usually sterilized before they are packaged in order to make them free of pathogens and disease-causing microorganisms. This is a good advantage as against using garden soil to plant.

c) **Lights & Reflective Hoods:** Selecting proper lighting and regulating it correctly is very important when growing cannabis indoors. The better and more consistent the light supply is, the more buds a plant will produce. The regular incandescent, halogen bulbs used commonly in homes is not appropriate for growing cannabis.
When growing seedlings and clones, fluorescent lights can be used, however, when the plants grow older, the light has to be changed to a more intensifying High-Intensity Discharge (HID) lights. They supply the appropriate illumination and heat to help plants grow into their vegetative as well as flowering stages.

Metal Halide and High-Pressure Sodium HIDs can either be in 400, 600 or 1,000 watts and as with other types of bulbs, the higher the wattage, the brighter the light it will emit as well as the more the electricity that would be required to power it. Metal Halide[9] emit light which is akin to sunlight so they are better for the vegetation phase while High-Pressure Sodium bulbs emit a yellowish orange light which is more suitable for flowering. Growers usually mix both of them in a grow room but if a grower wants to use just one type of lamp, the High-Pressure Sodium is usually the most preferred choice.

Also, the higher the wattage, the higher the lumen[10]. Metal Halide lamps usually have lower lumen in comparison to High-Pressure Sodium Lamps of the same wattage[11] which is why a High-Pressure sodium lamp is usually brighter than Metal Halide lamp of the same wattage.

The size of the grow room will determine the type, quality as well as quantity of bulbs needed for the plants in it. Lower wattage bulbs can be used in smaller rooms[12] and vice versa. Every quarter in a year, professional growers ca produce up to one pound of buds for every 1,000 watt bulb used. To optimize light consumption, it is always best to place a reflective hood over the HIDs in the grow room to ensure the light reflects directly onto the plants.[13]

Bulbs that are suitable for growing rooms are meant to mimic the sun and usually emit a lot of heat. When the weather outside is hot, particularly during summer, the heat in a grow room will intensify. Because of this, many indoor growers prefer using a basement as a grow room, particularly when the house has no air conditioning. The location of a basement is ideal for curbing heat.

d) **Electricity and Wiring:** A grow room would need to be wired for electricity to power the lights, fans, possibly the timers, and other equipment used in the room. If cannabis is grown in a house, it is usually done in an enclosed room. Because of this, it is important that safety is strictly adhered to when wiring a grow room.

Because the light in a grow room is usually higher in wattage than other domestic light bulbs within an average home, it is necessary to create a different circuit for the grow room which is separate from the wiring in the house. Electricity tariffs will naturally increase because of this.

Due to grow rooms typically being isolated and usually warm, particular care must be taken to ensure that naked wires are properly covered.

e) **Water:** Generous quantities of water from a good water supply will be needed in the grow room and tap water[14] will serve just fine. Well-water sometimes contains salt and should be avoided where possible. Water with a pH[15] level of between 6-8 is okay for growing cannabis. Adequate drainage channels will be required. Plumbing in the grow room should be such that water can easily be drained off and in areas where drainage pipes are impossible to install, trays or troughs can be placed to collect run-off water.

As cannabis plants mature, so does their need for water. Use of soilless mix also increases the need for water because soilless mix drains well. On the average, plants are usually watered every two days. The growing medium is fully saturated with water and when the water drains off and the medium is dry then the plant should be watered again. If plants are not watered frequently, they will become dehydrated and their leaves and branches fall downwards.

Many grow mediums are made with wetting agents[16] but a simple solution of water and some drops of household dish washing liquid will act as an effective wetting agent. Watering the plants should be done slowly and evenly around the root so the growing medium does not harden as one solid piece and leave spaces around the pot where water can escape.

Cannabis leaves and stems also need to be sprayed with water to imitate rain in normal environmental conditions. Misting is best done just before grow room lights are switched off to prevent rapid evaporation. This will help not only keep them moist but also remove dust from their surface and open the leaf pores.

One last thing to note is that the use of fertilizers and other chemicals will likely cause a buildup of salt residue eventually. This problem can be solved by watering the plant with about three times the normal quantity of water required some time after the use of fertilizers. The water cleans out the growing medium as it drains from the bottom of the pot.

f) **Ventilation:** Proper air ventilation cannot be compromised in a grow room because the cannabis plants (like all other plants) need carbon dioxide constantly. Air needs to be supplied and when it becomes stale, it needs to be removed.

Two primary vents that would be required are an air intake vent[17] to let in air and an exhaust vent[18] to expel air from the grow room. Depending on which part of the house the grow room is, it can be a bit tricky figuring out where to install vents but with a little creativity, it should not be too hard. Fans can be attached to the vents to help either with the expelling or the drawing in air.

Proper ventilation also helps curb odors. If the plant odors become so strong and the vents in the grow room and the use of air fresheners can't curb them, then an ozone generator can be used to curb odors drastically.[19] Though highly effective, ozone generators are expensive and might require additional construction. Alternatively, carbon filters can be attached to the exhaust fan to curb odors. They filter out odors in the charcoal within their filter along with the air being expelled. They are much easier to install and use than ozone generators.

Fans are needed to replace the wind which aids to stir leaves and stalks to become stronger as well as to ward off bugs and dust. Regardless of how thick the insulation around the grow room is, the noise of the fans will most likely be audible. Fans also do not camouflage the strong odors of the cannabis plants.

Bearing this in mind, the grower should think of alternative locations to establish the grow room if noise and odors will be intolerable at their location. As mentioned previously, some growers use their basements, backrooms, garages or garden sheds to avoid this inconvenience because these rooms are accessed less frequently and usually at a strategic location in the home where these problems can be tackled.

Alternatively, the design of the grow room can be enhanced by using double insulation on the walls to reduce noise and special filter boxes can also reduce odors. Baffle boxes can be fitted to the fans in order to muffle the noise from them.

g) **Timers:** Electronic and digital timers help the grower turn on and turn off the lights and pumps during the lifecycle of indoor grown cannabis plants. Timers can also be used to control the air vents and fans. There are several different types of timers. The most important thing is to ensure the one chosen is simple to operate and can be easily replaced if it wears out (which happens quite often).

h) **Thermometers:** Temperature of between 70 to 85 degrees Fahrenheit are best for grow rooms. This is equivalent to 20 – 30 degrees centigrade. The lights in the grow room will produce heat. The fans and the vents will also have an effect on the temperature. Again, depending on what season it is, the grow room temperature could either drop or increase. Summer is always the hottest.

Increasing or decreasing the air coming in through the vents as well as the fans, can help regulate temperature. In hot climates, some growers install air conditioners to help reduce heat during the hot seasons.

i) **Pests and disease:** Poor temperatures, ventilation, and humidity will encourage the growth of spider mites. Oscillating fans and maintaining average temperatures of 75 degrees Fahrenheit will help ward off insect pests.

In an eventual insect infestation, most farmers have discovered that spraying a light mixture of dish wash soap and water on the surface and the back of the cannabis leaves, is effective in curbing insects like spider mites.[20]Though pesticides can also be effective, most farmers avoid using it as much as possible. Some farmers even prefer natural insect control measures like introducing ladybugs into the grow room. If pesticides are used, they must never be sprayed on the buds of the plant.

Mold could also be a potential problem in cultivating cannabis plants. White mold and black mold infestations could pose a challenge if not handled properly. White molds are powdery and result from high humidity or spraying leaves with water (which is technically unavoidable). White molds can appear on the leaves any time during the lifecycle of the plant. Black and gray mold could appear when the in the later stage of the plant's lifecycle when the flower clusters are dense. They can also occur if the cannabis stalks are cut or damaged. They are harder to detect.

Additional Caution: A grow room must be kept clean, sterile and clutter free to prevent infestation or disease. Only items used frequently in maintaining the plants and the equipment should be left in the room. If any of this equipment is taken outside the grow room for use elsewhere, they should be sterilized before they are brought back into the grow room. Unsterilized equipment can introduce disease to the plants in a grow room. Even new equipment should be cleaned and sterilized before use in the grow room.

Certain clothes can be isolated for use in the grow room only. Carpets are generally unnecessary in grow rooms and when damp, they can as culture mediums for harmful microorganisms or insects. The floor of a grow room is best when stripped off of any carpeting and cleaned thoroughly with light bleach water. However, if the carpets must remain, then, they need to be cleaned, sterilized and properly covered with materials like plastic which can act as barriers to dampness.

With time, the plants will begin to shed leaves and water will start running off from the bottom of planting pots. These should not be allowed to accumulate in the grow room. They must be tidied regularly.

Appropriate humidity in a grow room should be between 40 and 60 percent. In extremely dry environments, a humidifier can be used and if the environment is the opposite, then a dehumidifier can be used.

Determining The Species

The indica species of cannabis is highly preferred by indoor growers for a number of reasons. First, it has a shorter growing period because it flowers quicker than other species so it can be cultivated more often within a growing period. Shorter growing periods also reduce the risk of exposure to disease in comparison to other varieties.

Obtaining Seeds

Several seed companies in countries with no legal restrictions on cannabis use, retail cannabis seeds. It is not hard to find a supplier online. The challenge is identifying a reputable one. Some of them also do not ship to the United States. Like other agricultural suppliers of plant seeds, you would need to conduct your own independent due diligence checks.

Prices vary across companies but the price is not usually a guarantee for quality. The company's reputation is a higher indicator or guarantee of the quality of seeds you will eventually receive. Local growers can also supply seeds but you will have to look for them within your local contacts or network

Germinating Cannabis Seeds

Cannabis seeds are quite small; usually about the size of the head of a matchstick. The first step when growing cannabis is sprouting the seeds. Different people achieve this in different ways.

Sprouting Method 1:
Place seeds in distilled water for twenty-four hours. When the seeds are examined, they will have a white tiny root pushing out of one end. This means they have sprouted. The water can be strained and seeds that have not sprouted at this point can be discarded. All healthy seeds can then be transferred to a growing medium.

Sprouting Method 2:
Spread a few layers of paper kitchen towels or tissue on a flat surface like a tray and moisten them with water to create a sprouting medium. Distribute the seeds evenly around the surface of the tray. Just ensure that they are not too clustered together. Place the tray on an elevated surface and leave the seeds to sprout.

Sprouting Method 3:
Many cannabis growers prefer sprouting method 2 but there are a number of them who adopt a different approach. They prepare a tray or bed of soil instead of paper towels. The seeds are then placed about half an inch to an inch deep in the grow soil and left to sprout.

Whatever method is used, there are a couple of important things to note. First, ensure that the tray with seeds is not left on the bare floor afterward. The cold temperature from the ground might inhibit their growth. The tray must be kept on an elevated surface, which is best for promoting warm temperatures, necessary for sprouting.

The next most important thing to remember is covering sprouting seeds with a moisture or humidity dome. Some of these are sold in the gardening sections of large retail stores and come along with custom made growing trays. They are usually made of transparent plastic to prevent the escape of moisture from the growing medium, allowing light into the plant, protecting the delicate seedlings from harsh environmental conditions as well as enable the grower to observe the plant. Where not available, improvising with other suitable things is an option. Sprouts will shoot up in about three to four days.

Alternative Sprouting Method: Clones i.e. Cuttings

Apart from cultivating cannabis plants through their seeds, another way of growing them is through cloning. Clones are simply cuts or clippings taken out of mature plants so every clone is genetically identical to the parent plant from which it was cut from.

As explained in the section about the anatomy of the cannabis plant, the female, unpollinated, seedless cannabis plants are of more economic value than the male plants because of their buds. This is why feminized cannabis seeds are more desirable. However, it is not always guaranteed that only feminized seeds will be available from the company you are purchasing seeds from. In order to maximize a grower's profit as well as optimize growing time and resources, clones are usually taken from female unpollinated plants.

Cutting cannabis clones is quite technical for a number of reasons. A cannabis farmer's first challenge is identifying whether the plant from which the clones need to be taken is male or female. Determining the sex of a plant can only be done after pollination because only then will the females sprout their recognizable flowers. However, remember that a female plant that has been pollinated will eventually produce seeds and seeds are only required for replanting. They are not of any value to the end consumer. Cannabis growers overcome this challenge through two methods.

Determining The Sex Of A Cannabis Plant (Method 1):

In a controlled environment of growing room, cannabis growers simulate natural growing conditions using technology. For example, electric lights replace sunlight, fans generate wind and sprinklers provide water. Electric lights in a growing room are very important equipment. They are adjusted to glow at certain times and turned off or dimmed at certain periods to emulate different seasons in the normal seasons in the environment. These periods are technically referred to as photoperiods.

Prior to pollination, a cannabis plant would only need 18 hours of light and 6 hours of darkness. To kick start pollination, growers adjust the light setting to 12 hours of light and 12 hours of darkness. Adjusting lights in the grow room to only 12 hours mimics the atmospheric conditions of late summer and prompts budding in the cannabis plants. When the plants show the first signs of budding, the farmer quickly isolates the female plants from the rest and places them back under the earlier 18 hours light and 6-hour darkness conditions.

Doing this will make the plants revert back to their pre-budding state and once they do so, clones are clipped from the female plants and then replanted. This method gives a hundred percent guarantee that all the future cannabis plants grown will be female and of the species. The only catch is that when a plant is prompted to bud and then reversed back to its former state, it might get stressed and eventually end up being unusable.

Determining The Sex Of A Cannabis Plant (Method 2):

The second way of getting desired female clones is to randomly cut clones prior to when plants are about to bud and replant them in grow mediums and then allow the parent plants to continue budding. The clones will have to be properly marked in order to easily identify which plant they originally were cut from.

When the parent plant buds, and it is female, the clones taken from it can definitely be confirmed as female. The female clones (which would not have reached any significant maturity stage) are then separated and groomed to continue growing till maturity.

If the parent plant is male, the clones from the male parent plant are destroyed saving the grower any time and effort that would have been expended in growing them.

To make the roots of a clone sprout faster, plant growth hormones are usually dabbed on the blades of the sharp knives used to cut clones. Seedlings could also be crown with a light mixture of 20-20-20 fertilizer until they reach a vegetative state.

Growth Cycle Of The Cannabis Plant

If cannabis is grown indoors i.e. inside a grow room, it takes approximately eleven to twelve weeks i.e. three to four months before a cannabis seedling grows to a fully mature plant for harvesting. Some growers can stretch the growing cycle for as much as six to eight months or more from germination to maturity.

Its growth cycle might take longer if the plant is grown outdoors because environmental conditions such as light cannot be controlled so the grower will be at the mercy of Mother Nature. More advanced, high-tech growing methods like hydroponics or aeroponics, will take shorter periods as water and nutrition are directly supplied to the plant in addition to light.

There are several reasons why the growth cycle could be shorter or longer. The reasons could range from the type of cannabis strain planted, how tall the grower wants the plant to be, how long the plants left in their flowering state before they are eventually harvested and other factors relating to the way they are grown, for example, the grow medium, type of fertilizer used, lighting conditions and other circumstances.

The time required for setting up equipment in the grow room and ordering of seeds or clones[21] could take somewhere between one to four weeks. This time should also be factored in particularly for first-time growers. Use of clones also saves the grower some time and shortens the growing period.

Seedling

STANDARD 2 – 6 WEEKS {Temperature 70-85F, Photoperiod 18 hours Light: 6 Hours Darkness} Seeds or clones are usually planted smaller pots or block of growing mediums. After about two to three weeks, the seedlings would begin to establish adequate roots and leaves that will enable them to move into the vegetative stage.

In about four weeks to six weeks, most seedlings would have grown enough to be transplanted into a bigger pot in which they will continue growing till they are harvested. Bigger pots[22] offer the needed space for their roots to grow and modify. All grow pots should have holes in the bottom to help drain off excess water.

Vegetative Stage

STANDARD 2 – 6 WEEKS {Temperature 70-85F, Photoperiod 18 hours Light: 6 Hours Darkness} The vegetative stage for cannabis usually ranges from two weeks to about two months. The shorter or longer it takes is a decision the grower makes. Some growers want very tall plants so that they can eventually harvest bigger buds so they leave the plant for much longer i.e. four or more weeks. Other growers want to quickly harvest the plant and start growing a new batch of plants. They typically would not allow their plants exceed a two to three weeks to a maximum of one month in the vegetative stage.

Fertilizers with high nitrogen content are usually required during the plants vegetative stage. Fertilizer application will be required after two or three watering periods.

In a vegetative state, the lights in the grow room are left on for a maximum of six (6) hours and kept off for eighteen (18) hours.

Flowering/ Budding/ Blooming

STANDARD 8 – 12 WEEKS {Temperature 70-85F, Photoperiod 12 hours light: 12 hours darkness} Six weeks to four months. At this stage, the flowers become dense and form buds on the tops of the plant's branches. The leaves also become coated with gummy resins, which have a content of tetrahydrocannabinol. While indica strains will take about seven to eight weeks to bud, sativa strains will take much longer.

A fertilizer that is high in phosphorous is appropriate during the flowering stage of cannabis. A high nitrogen fertilizer at this stage will cause rapid foliage to grow. Fertilizer application will be at the same rate as during the vegetative period.

After the flowering stage, the plants will be ready for harvesting.

Harvest

Most of the cannabis buds actually fully develop within two weeks during harvest. The change in color of the pistils or white hairs to orange to brownish red is the most significant physical indicator of the buds being ready for harvest. When mature plants are left for too long, they could attract mold infestation.

The topmost flowers will usually mature faster than those at the bottom. Growers use pruning shears to cut and trim[23] the cannabis flowers. The fan leaves are trimmed and the plants are graded according to their strains then they are manicured by removing the excess leaves around their colas to enable them to dry quickly.

After trimming, the buds are either hung to dry or placed on screens in a dark, well-ventilated room to dry. It takes about two to ten days[24] before buds are completely dried. Sometimes, cannabis buds might appear dry but still be wet inside. Cannabis growers will usually place the buds in a sealed polythene bag or container and leave it for a couple of hours to redistribute the water in the bud. When taken out, if they are wet, the buds are then spread out or hung again to dry and the process is repeated until they are thoroughly dried.

This process of re-distributing any water is known as 'sweating' or 'curing'[25]. Buds are thoroughly dry when they are sweated and do not come out wet but still remain dry. At this point, the buds are said to be fully 'cured'. Cured, dried buds can be stashed away in Ziploc bags, airtight or compressed jars for future use. They are best preserved in a dark, cold storage area.

Cultivating Cannabis Through Hydroponics

The cutting edge, high tech platform hydroponic farming offers, is soaring in popularity among modern day farmers for very good reasons. Hydroponic farming is highly efficient because it cuts out a lot of time wasting and energy sapping systems in other common farming methods. It requires less space and avails a neater, more sanitary method of farming which greatly reduces disease.

Hydroponics farming is also quite low maintenance but ironically, gives the farmer a high degree of control and delivers crop yield that is reported to be 100% more than other known farming techniques. There are different types[26] of hydroponic systems but all of them would usually contain four main elements:

   a) A basin or PVC pipe in which pots containing grow mediums, which may be mineral, based pellets or fibers are placed. These pots will hold the root of the plant. Alternatively, baskets containing pellets or grow mediums could be used for individual plants and they are placed in the basin.
   b) A water reservoir (usually below the basin)
   c) A pump to aerate the water reservoir.
   d) A water cycle is established when water is pumped into the basin and from the reservoir and it drains back into the basin.

More sophisticated hydroponics systems will pump water with a timer but the others will just pump water slowly across the system. Alternative power supply arrangements like an electricity generator and a water pump, need to be made particularly for hydroponic systems that do not use grow mediums but require water pumped at intervals.[27]

The water in the reservoir is usually referred to as the 'nutrient solution' and it needs to have the appropriate pH[28], temperature[29], and fertilizer[30] for the cannabis plant. The nutrient solution can change during the plant's lifecycle so they must be monitored with meters and if any change is noticed, steps should be taken to curb it.

Cannabis buds harvested under a hydroponics system are usually larger in size. The initial knowledge of operating a hydroponics system could be a bit intensive until it is understood, it will be very easy for the grower to implement. The effort expended to cultivate cannabis plants (or any other plants) in a hydroponics system is usually far lower than traditional methods of farming. Care, however, must be taken when using a hydroponic system as plants can be very sensitive to any adverse conditions.

When cannabis is grown outdoors or indoors, the soil or soilless mix provides a foundational structure for the roots to hold on to. A hydroponics farm eliminates the use of these basic foundations and provides nutrients directly to the root through water in addition to providing oxygen directly to the root through aeration. The availability of oxygen at root level speeds the plants nutritional intake, which in turn hastens the cannabis plant growth and the bud production.

Clones grown in Rockwell cubes are usually more preferred when growing in a hydroponic system because they can be easily placed in the pot, basket or PVC pipe to continue growing. The fibers in Rockwell cubes also allow free passage of water to the roots.

Lighting conditions in hydroponic systems will be the same as that in indoor cultivation. The total growth life cycle will be shorter and harvesting will also be earlier.

Outdoor Cannabis Cultivation

Often times, people forget that like most weeds, cannabis grows in the wild and has been cultivated outdoors for thousands of years before indoor and hydroponics farming started becoming popular. Outdoor grown cannabis is actually said to have richer aromas, deeper flavors, and better taste than those grown through any other method.

Cannabis grows all over the world and the two strains i.e. indica and sativa are well adapted to temperate and tropical climates respectively. Growers located in the Northern Hemisphere would typically from between April to October.

Cannabis that grows in the open would naturally be pollinated and its seeds dispersed through natural agents like the wind. These seeds find their way back into the soil and regrow to naturally replenish the plant population.

There are many challenges with outdoor farming and it discourages a lot of potential growers except when it is the only option. The natural environmental conditions cannot be controlled. And security cannot be guaranteed. Both humans and animals can stumble into an outdoor garden and either destroy it or help themselves to your hard labor. In areas where there are cannabis restriction laws, your farm can be put on surveillance and you would be arrested. Nevertheless, cannabis is still grown outdoors in many parts of the globe.

Outdoor cannabis farming is a challenge for people who live in temperate parts of the world. Cannabis thrives on light. While growers who live in the tropics might be able to grow cannabis at least twice a year, those who live in temperate regions may only be able to grow cannabis during the hotter part of the year.

Choosing A Site: An appropriate and convenient site needs to be selected for outdoor cultivation. Sites can range from a simple back garden to a remote place in the forest where there is a little or no intrusion of security on the cannabis garden. Growers who farm in the forest are typically 'guerilla' farmers who do so to hide their operations. Some growers even place soil in bags and hoist them on trees. The proximity of the site chosen will determine how frequent the plants can be visited or observed. It will also be good to test the soil in the chosen site for acidity and alkalinity. The pH should be as neutral as possible and not excessive.

Sites that have no objects blocking exposure to sunlight e.g. buildings, trees, hills, etc. are best. The site is cleared and the planting beds raised at least 6 to 8 inches above the ground. When the beds are prepared, some farmers will gather compost material like grass, leaves, vegetative matter, branches, etc. on the beds and allow it to rot. Site preparation outdoors could take at least a month and even as much as six months before seedlings or clones are ready for planting.

Transplanting Seedling & Clones: Seedling or clones may be used and if the soil in the chosen site is tough, then arrangements for watering the plants will need to be made, particularly in the early growth stages. Seedlings are usually sprouted indoors. Cannabis growers usually sprout more seeds than the intended number of plants they actually want to grow because seeds might likely not survive outdoors. It is better to sprout seeds under normal outdoor conditions. Change from artificial indoor light can be harsh to them. However, if seeds must be sprouted indoors, a gradual acclimatization to sunlight will be necessary. This can start by keeping them in shaded areas before gradually introducing them to direct sunlight. The white sprouts of germinated seeds can be put about a quarter to half an inch inside the soil and then left to continue growing. Transplanting seedlings or clones are best done by mid-April when the days are longer than the nights so that flowering will not be induced too early.

Sunlight: An outdoor grower has no control over light. If the site is near the home, some outdoor growers erect bulbs at strategic areas so that the plant can be tricked to remain in its vegetative state by shining light directly on them for a couple of extra hours.

Water Supply: The drier the soil, the more water you will need during outdoor growing. Guerilla farmers, in particular, use sites located near streams, rivers or lakes. Alternatives would be providing alternative water sources like a water tank with watering hose, watering can or irrigation systems. As the plants grow bigger, especially during their vegetative stage, they require water more.

Fertilization: With respect to fertilizer application, organic fertilizers like animal droppings, blood meal, bone meal, worm castings, etc., are a favorite for outdoor growers. Chemical fertilizers with higher Nitrogen ratio in comparison to Phosphorous and Potassium e.g. 5:1:1 is also great where organic fertilizers are not available. Over fertilization should be avoided. Fertilizer must be used according to guidelines and plants observed for any unusual changes during fertilizer application.

Weeding & Pest Control: Weeds have to be taken out frequently so that the plants are not deprived of the essential nutrients weeds are competing for. Manually taking out weeds is best. Weed killers could have adverse effects on the plant.

Pests could greatly vary outdoors; From insects (like spider mites, mealybugs, whiteflies) to birds and animals. Pests are a bigger threat when the plants are younger. Companion planting with strong smelling plants like mint, cloves, garlic, cayenne pepper can help ward off pests. Some natural predators like ladybugs, birds, and frogs also feed on insect pests. Natural homemade pesticides made with regular dish washing soap and garlic extract are very effective. Fences can also help keep off animals.

Winds: Wind can be a threat to cannabis grown outdoors so a couple of measures can be taken to protect cannabis plants from wind damage. First, other plants can be grown around them to act as windbreakers. The problem with this method is that these plants might compete with the cannabis plants for water and nutrients in the soil. Second, wood or metal stakes can be driven into the ground then the plants are tied close to the stakes. A third method would be to construct a fence around the plants. Velcro, string, trellis netting, wire tomato cages and extendable wire are all used to support cannabis plants at different stages of growth.

Harvest: Abundance of orange-red pistils are usually an indication that plants are ready for harvest. When buds are finally harvested, they can also be dried outside under an enclosure or tent, which can be set, up to protect the buds and help them dry faster. Better still, the branches can be trimmed or the plants pulled out and dried indoors.

Some growers leave the male cannabis plants so that they can flower and pollinate the females to produce seeds for replanting. A balance needs to be created by not pulling out plants too early. Opening up their sheaths or bracts to check for a marbling brown color will let you know if they are ready for harvest or not. The harvest and curing procedure is typically the same like that of those grown indoors.

Conclusion

Every cannabis cultivation method is unique and results will be different for every farmer. It is necessary to continually research for better ways of improving on the farming method a grower chooses as well as crop yields.

This book has offered you an essential insight into growing cannabis but, a lot of information is available online and at local libraries. There is countless cannabis growing blogs, websites, and forums where growers interact to share their experiences. It is also necessary to look for local farmers, observe their techniques and exchange information. Different localities offer different advantages and challenges that the residents are familiar with.

As mentioned earlier on, every grower will need to check and comply with the laws governing cannabis use and cultivation in their area before embarking on a cannabis growing project. Growing cannabis illegally poses a huge risk to the grower.

The process of growing your own cannabis can be exciting and rewarding. Once you grow the first one, even if it is only one plant, from seed to harvest, subsequent ones will become easier as you build on your previous experience to cultivate better yields.

Thank you so much for purchasing my book and if this book was insightful and added any value to you, please leave a quick review on Amazon.com

All The Best☺

Endnotes

[1] Around 2737BC
[2] Also known as 'hash'.
[3] These pipes are also called hookahs, bongs, bubblers or hot knifepoints.
[4] The movie, 'Reefer Madness' was released in 1936 to show that cannabis use could lead to rape, murder, and other unthinkable crimes.
[5] Bill Clinton, George W. Bush and Barrack Obama all admitted to using cannabis.
[6] This shorter maturity period makes the indica species a favourite for indoor growers.
[7] Soilless mixes are made up of:
   a) Peat moss: Usually coarse but lightweight and sterile. Can hold water well particularly when mixed with other growing mediums.
   b) Perlite: Expanded volcanic rock which is usually white in colour.
   c) Vermiculite: A form of mica which holds water but provides aeration as well. (Phillips, 2015)

If components of the soil mix are bought separately then, all three of them can be mixed in equal parts or equal quantities of peat moss and perlite will do. A little lime will need to be added to moderate the soil mix's pH level.

[8] Cannabis requires the following nutrients:
   a) Nitrogen
   b) Phosphorous
   c) Potassium
   d) Calcium
   e) Magnesium
   f) Manganese
   g) Boron
   h) Zinc
   i) Sulphur
   j) Iron
   k) Molybdenum
   l) Copper

Both chemical and organic fertilizers will indicate the proportion on nutrients they contain on their labelling. Three numbers like 10-15-5 tell the percentage proportion Nitrogen, Phosphorous and Potassium contained in the fertilizer. The higher the percentage of the chemical, the higher the dilution that would be required before the fertilizer is applied to the plant. The other trace nutrients will also be written on the label.

[9] Metal Halide lamps will require their own special sockets, electricity circuit and ballast. The regular domestic light bulb sockets cannot accommodate HIDs. Installing them will also increase daily electricity consumption.

[10] Lumen refers to the measurable quantity of visible light emitted by a source of light. It is sometimes shortened as 'lm'.

[11] A 400 watt metal halide bulb will have a lumen of approximately 19,000lm while a 400 watt High Pressure Sodium bulb will have a lumen of 32,000lm. This is almost thirty percent (30%) more lumen.

[12] The guide for light in grow rooms are:
   a) 5-12 square feet – 250 watts
   b) 8-20 square feet – 400 watts
   c) 12-30 square feet – 600 watts
   d) 20-50 square feet – 1,000 watts

[13] A distance of 1 foot is recommended for 250 watt lamps while 1,000 watt lamps can be kept About 1.25 – 2.5 feet away from the plants. As the plant grows, it increases in height so growers usually either adjust the light itself or the height of the plant to maintain a good distance between both.

[14] Some growers place water in a container overnight to allow the chlorine to evaporate before they use it on the plants. Farmers who use the water straight from the tap do not report any adverse effects from the chlorine content.

[15] If the pH level is unsuitable, a pH adjuster (which is usually sold in stores) can be used to adjust it.
[16] Wetting agents help prevent the build-up of dry pockets in the grow medium.
[17] To let in air from outside into the room
[18] Usually placed in the ceiling to transport air out of the house.
[19] Ozone generators work by breaking down the microorganisms which cause odors.
[20] If the solution is too soapy, another follow up spray of fresh, clean water should be done after twenty four hours to clean the leaves and open up their pores.

[21] In the United States (Haze)
[22] The general rule of thumb for selecting the size of a pot is one gallon for each foot of the plant height. For example, a grower who wants a three-foot plant would require a three gallon pot. Grow pots are usually about three to eight gallons large.
[23] It is best to trim once the buds are cut off from the plant. If done later, the leaves would be limp and harder to cut.
[24] i.e. two weeks or more depending on the grower
[25] Buds are sometimes cured for about half the time they are dried. SO they could be dried for about 40 hours and cured for a15 – 20 hours.
[26] Top Feed hydroponic systems, Ebb & Flow aka Flood and Drain hydroponic systems, Nutrient Film Technique (NFT) hydroponic systems (no grow medium used)
[27] A typical example would be the NFT system.
[28] 5.9 to 6.3 is the appropriate pH for hydroponic systems water and pH test strips or digital meters can be used to test pH level at frequent intervals.
[29] 68 to 77 degrees Fahrenheit is the recommended temperature for water in hydroponic systems. This can be monitored with swimming pool or digital thermometers. An aquarium heater can be used to raise the temperature of the water when it drops and it the temperature rises, the water can be passed through a cooling rack first before it gets to the plants. Passing hoses or pipes with cold water running through them in the reservoir, can also help cool down the water's temperature.
[30] Hydroponic solutions are liquid fertilizers. Fertilizer concentration of 700-1,600ppm is best for cannabis. Ppm or 'parts per meter' is measured with an EC (Electrical Conductivity) meter.

Works Cited

Advanced Holistic Health (AHH). (n.d.). *10,000-year History of Marijuana use in the World*. Retrieved January 12, 2016, from AdvancedHolisticHealth.org: http://www.advancedholistichealth.org/history.html

Bailey, R. (2014, September 6). *Cannabis Anatomy: the Parts of the Plant*. Retrieved January 10, 2016, from Leafy.com: https://www.leafly.com/news/cannabis-101/cannabis-anatomy-the-parts-of-the-plant

Bergman, R. (2014, May 8). *Protect Your Outdoor Marijuana Plants From Wind Damage*. Retrieved January 16, 2016, from TheWeedBlog.com: http://www.theweedblog.com/protect-your-outdoor-marijuana-plants-from-wind-damage/

Bergman, R. (2015, October 8). *The Difference Between Indica, Sativa And Hybrid*. Retrieved January 16, 2016, from ILoveGrowingMarijuana.com: http://www.ilovegrowingmarijuana.com/difference-indica-sativa-hybrid/

Borchardt, D. (2016, January 7). *Cannabis Conferences Are Growing Like Weeds*. Retrieved January 8, 2016, from Forbes.com: http://www.forbes.com/sites/debraborchardt/2016/01/07/cannabis-conferences-are-growing-like-weeds/

Dutch Passion Seed Company. (n.d.). *Growing cannabis Outdoors*. Retrieved January 16, 2015, from Dutch-Passion.nl: http://www.dutch-passion.nl/en/grow-info/growing-cannabis-outdoors/

Green, G. (2001). *The Cannabis Grow Bible*.

Haze, N. (n.d.). *How Long Does It Take to Grow Weed?* Retrieved January 14, 2015, from GrowWeedEasy.com: http://www.growweedeasy.com/how-long-does-it-take-to-grow-weed

Jackel. (2012, September 2). *10 Tips For Growing Outdoors*. Retrieved January 16, 2015, from MarijuanaGrowersHQ.com: http://www.marijuanagrowershq.com/10-tips-for-growing-outdoor/

Phillips, N. (2015, November 2). *Soiless Potting Mix - What Is A Soilless Mixture And Making Homemade Soilless Mix*. Retrieved January 12, 2016, from GardeningKnowHow.com: http://www.gardeningknowhow.com/garden-how-to/soil-fertilizers/soilless-growing-mediums.htm

Rowley, L. (2015, October 5). *Where Is Marijuana Legal in the United States? List of Recreational and Medicinal States*. Retrieved January 16, 2016, from Mic.com: http://mic.com/articles/126303/where-is-marijuana-legal-in-the-united-states-list-of-recreational-and-medicinal-states#.3Lf92Qs0Y

Royal Queen Seeds. (2014, August 25). *10 Tips for Growing Cannabis*. Retrieved January 11, 2016, from RoyalQueenSeeds.com: http://www.royalqueenseeds.com/blog-10-tips-for-growing-cannabis-n97

Smart, B. (2014, December 30). *Comparing common methods of supporting plants*. Retrieved January 16, 2016, from MarijuanaVenture.com: http://www.marijuanaventure.com/comparing-common-methods-supporting-plants/

Made in the USA
San Bernardino, CA
17 April 2018